# THE ANIMAL FILES
# WE NEED
# BATS

by Christopher Forest

FOCUS READERS

# WWW.FOCUSREADERS.COM

Focus Readers is distributed by North Star Editions:
sales@northstareditions.com | 888-417-0195

Produced for Focus Readers by Red Line Editorial.

Content Consultant: Dr. Scott M. Bergeson, Visiting Assistant Professor of Biology, Purdue University Fort Wayne

Photographs ©: CraigRJD/iStockphoto, cover, 1; Sura Nualpradid/Shutterstock Images, 4–5; Red Line Editorial, 6, 29; Merlin D. Tuttle/Science Source, 8, 15; gallimaufry/Shutterstock Images, 10–11; Pichai Tunsuphon/Shutterstock Images, 12; Michael Lynch/Shutterstock Images, 17; Warren Metcalf/Shutterstock Images, 18–19; Hendrasu/Shutterstock Images, 21; Jay Ondreicka/Shutterstock Images, 23; Thomas Males/Shutterstock Images, 24–25; Elena Avilova/Shutterstock Images, 27

**Library of Congress Cataloging-in-Publication Data**
Names: Forest, Christopher, author.
Title: We need bats / by Christopher Forest.
Description: Lake Elmo, MN : Focus Readers, [2019] | Series: The animal files
  | Audience: Grade 4 to 6. | Includes index.
Identifiers: LCCN 2018035055 (print) | LCCN 2018036363 (ebook) | ISBN
  9781641854832 (PDF) | ISBN 9781641854252 (e-book) | ISBN 9781641853095
  (hardcover) | ISBN 9781641853675 (paperback)
Subjects: LCSH: Bats--Ecology--Juvenile literature. |
  Bats--Conservation--Juvenile literature.
Classification: LCC QL737.C5 (ebook) | LCC QL737.C5 F66 2019 (print) | DDC
  599.4--dc23
LC record available at https://lccn.loc.gov/2018035055

Printed in the United States of America
Mankato, MN
October, 2018

# ABOUT THE AUTHOR

Christopher Forest is a middle-school teacher in Massachusetts. In his free time, he enjoys writing books for all ages. He has written nonfiction and fiction stories, articles, and novels. He also enjoys watching sports, playing guitar, reading, and spending time outdoors.

# TABLE OF CONTENTS

# CHAPTER 1

# THE NIGHT VISITOR

The sky darkens as the sun sets. A light wind blows through the trees. Soon, a dark shadow appears in the sky. At first, the shadow looks like a bird. It darts between trees, as if chasing something. Then it swoops down low. The shadow has a furry face and large, pointed ears.

A swarm of bats in Thailand sets out to hunt.

These traits leave no doubt. The night visitor is a bat.

Bats live in all parts of the globe, except for Earth's polar regions. In total, there are more than 1,200 bat **species**.

## A WORLD OF BATS

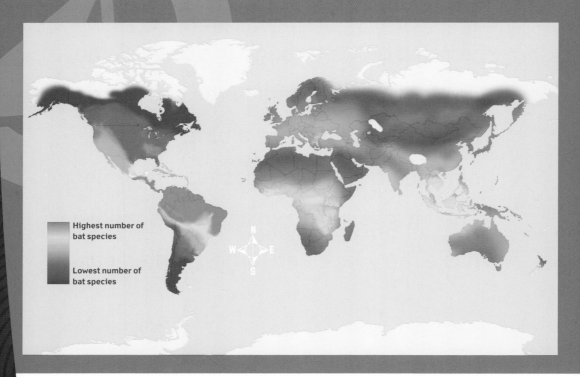

Highest number of bat species

Lowest number of bat species

N
W E
S

Bats live in forests, mountains, farmland, and cities. Most species prefer warm weather. But some species live in Alaska and other cold places.

Bats are nocturnal. This means they sleep during the day. At night, bats take to the sky in search of food. Many bats eat insects. Some bats prefer **nectar** or fruit. Others eat birds, fish, and even other bats.

Bats use their strong sense of hearing to find their **prey**. One little brown bat can eat up to 500 mosquitoes in an hour. Bats are the top nighttime **predator** of insects. They help keep insect populations under control.

A Mehely's horseshoe bat catches a moth in its mouth.

Bats are very important to local **ecosystems**. Thanks to bats, there are fewer insects to destroy plants and crops. However, many people dislike bats. These animals come out at night. They dart and swoop. Sometimes, they fly into homes. People may also be afraid of bats' ratlike faces. Some bat species bite animals and lap their blood. They may carry diseases. For these reasons, bats get a bad name. Many people do not understand the animals' benefits.

## ECHOLOCATION

It is a myth that bats are blind. Even though several species are **color-blind**, all bats can see. Bats hunt at night, so they rely on many senses as they fly. They also use echolocation. When bats echolocate, they use sound to find objects. First, the bat makes a sound through its mouth or nose. Then, it listens for the sound to bounce back, or echo, off an object. This ability helps the bat find its way in the dark.

# CHAPTER 2

# SERVING THE ECOSYSTEM

**B**ats are more than predators. They are also pollinators. A pollinator is an animal that carries pollen from plant to plant. Pollen is a fine powder made by some plants. When bats spread pollen, plants can make new fruit or seeds. Many plant species rely on bats for pollination.

A fruit bat hangs in a banana tree in Sri Lanka.

Kapok buds stay closed during the day and open at night.

For instance, bats are key pollinators of the saguaro cactus and the kapok tree. They also pollinate bananas and cacao. Plants that rely on bats typically have flowers that bloom at night. Bats visit these plants to eat fruits, insects, and nectar. As a bat eats, the plant's pollen sticks to its fur. The bat then spreads the pollen when it flies to other plants.

Bats also help spread the seeds of plants and trees. Many tropical bats live on a diet of fruit. These bats release the fruit's seeds in their waste, which is called guano. The guano serves as a **fertilizer** for the seeds. It allows the seeds to grow quickly and easily.

Many rain forests have been harmed by human activity. Humans clear plants and trees to grow crops and build houses. However, bats' guano helps keep habitats healthy. Guano helps new trees grow.

For this reason, some people call bats the "farmers of the tropics." Humans even use guano as fertilizer in many parts of the world.

Guano is especially important for cave habitats. Caves are home to a variety of animals. Examples include amphibians, insects, and rats. Some of these animals rely on bat guano. The guano provides key nutrients the animals need to survive. Without bats, other species could die out. This could cause the entire ecosystem to fall apart.

A world without bats would be quite different. Insect populations would rise. Some plants would go extinct.

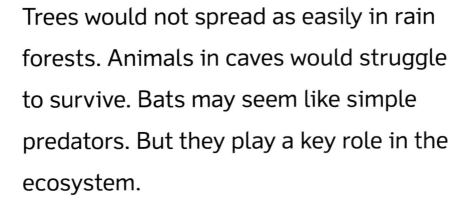

Some farmers use nets to collect guano.

Trees would not spread as easily in rain forests. Animals in caves would struggle to survive. Bats may seem like simple predators. But they play a key role in the ecosystem.

# VAMPIRE MEDICINE

Vampire bats are best known for their diet. They are the only mammal that feeds entirely on blood. They feed mainly on cow and chicken blood. Soon, vampire bats may be known for more than what they eat. They are helping scientists create a new medicine.

Vampire bats have a chemical in their spit that keeps blood from **clotting**. This chemical allows the bats to lap up blood more easily. Scientists collected samples of the spit while the bats were sleeping. Then they used the chemical in the spit to make Draculin. This medicine may be able to help people who have had strokes. A stroke can occur if blood clots inside a blood vessel leading to the brain. The clot stops the person's blood flow. Strokes can lead to brain injury or death.

Draculin keeps blood from clotting. It can also break up clots. Then blood can flow to the brain

Vampire bats live in caves and other dark places throughout Central and South America.

again. Scientists still need to study Draculin further. But one day, it could help save people's lives.

# CHAPTER 3

# THREATS TO BATS

**B**ats need healthy habitats to live and thrive. But in recent decades, habitat loss has posed a threat to bats. This means bats have fewer places to roost, or nest. They also have less food to eat. As a result, nearly one-third of bat species are threatened or endangered. If a species is endangered, it's at risk of dying off.

Long-nosed bats form the shape of a snake on a tree to scare off predators.

Habitat loss is often caused by humans. Humans destroy natural habitats to build homes, roads, and farms. Some of these habitats, such as forests, pond areas, and **hedgerows**, are important to bats. In many cases, humans cut down trees where bats roost. Habitat loss makes it difficult for bats to raise their young.

Cave destruction is another threat to bats. Many bats live in caves or mines. Some caves are home to millions of bats. However, caves and mines can be dangerous for humans. For this reason, people sometimes close off these spaces. But when caves are closed, bats can't return to their homes. People who explore

Fruit bats roost in the Monfort Bat Sanctuary in the Philippines.

caves can also cause problems. They might disturb bats that are **hibernating**. Constant waking in the winter can kill bats. It forces the bats to use valuable energy. They might not have enough energy left to survive until spring.

Some bats roost in buildings during the day. But the humans who use these buildings can disturb the bats. The bats may need to find new homes. Being disturbed while hibernating or raising babies can cause bat populations to decline.

## WHITE-NOSE SYNDROME

Disease is a major threat to bats. In 2006, a disease called white-nose syndrome broke out among bats in a cave in New York. The disease spread across the United States and Canada. White-nose syndrome damages bats' wings. It also causes bats to wake more often during hibernation. Between 2006 and 2012, the disease killed more than six million bats in North America.

A wildlife biologist checks a big brown bat for signs of white-nose syndrome.

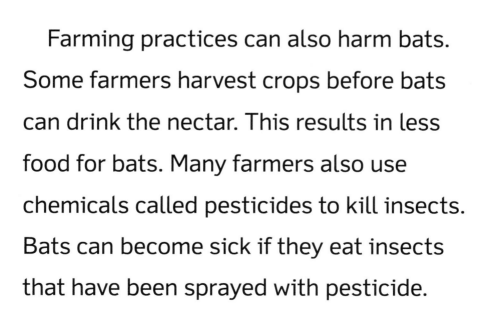

Farming practices can also harm bats. Some farmers harvest crops before bats can drink the nectar. This results in less food for bats. Many farmers also use chemicals called pesticides to kill insects. Bats can become sick if they eat insects that have been sprayed with pesticide.

# CHAPTER 4

# SAVING BATS

Conservationists are people who protect plants, animals, and natural resources. Conservationists are making efforts to save bat populations. For instance, some conservation groups raise awareness about the benefits of bats. They spread information and collect money to fund bat research.

People can help bats by hanging bat houses in trees.

Other groups rescue injured bats and create bat sanctuaries. A sanctuary is a safe, protected place where bats can live.

Individuals can also play a role in saving bats. Farmers can limit their use of pesticides. Families can call a professional to safely remove a bat if it enters a home. Families can also put bat houses in trees. These houses provide shelter to bats whose habitats have been destroyed.

Families can also help bats by planting night gardens. Night gardens are filled with plants that bloom or release scents at night. Some night gardens have flowers, such as evening primrose and

Many types of evening primrose flowers release scents at night.

white jasmine. Others have herbs, such as mint and lemon balm. These plants attract insects, which then attract bats.

Lawmakers can assist bats, too. They can pass laws that protect bat habitats. Many countries have laws that help bats.

For example, the United States has a law called the Endangered Species Act. This law makes it illegal to harm animals on the Endangered Species List.

Without bats, ecosystems would suffer. Trees in rain forests would not grow back

## GOING BATTY

Some people have jobs protecting bats. For example, sound surveyors use equipment to measure bats' echolocation calls. These calls help sound surveyors identify different bat species in a habitat. Other people become bat field technicians. These workers study bat populations in large areas, such as national parks. Sometimes, they work with colleges to study bats. The more scientists know about bats, the more they can help them.

as quickly. And there would be fewer animals to pollinate plants. By protecting bats, people help many other species thrive.

# SAVING A BAT SPECIES

The lesser long-nosed bat made a comeback from near extinction.

**1997 TO 2007:**
Conservationists work to protect plants that the bats eat.

**2015:**
Mexico removes the bat from its endangered species list.

1990     2000     2010     2020

**1988:**
Fewer than 1,000 lesser long-nosed bats live in the United States and Mexico. Both countries add the species to their endangered species lists.

**2007:**
The number of lesser long-nosed bats rises to 100,000.

**2018:**
More than 200,000 lesser long-nosed bats live in the United States and Mexico. This species is the first bat to be removed from the US Endangered Species List.

# FOCUS ON
# BATS

*Write your answers on a separate piece of paper.*

1. Write a paragraph describing one of the threats mentioned in Chapter 3.

2. Would you rather be a bat field technician or sound surveyor? Why?

3. Which sense do bats rely on most to fly and catch prey?
   
   **A.** sight
   **B.** touch
   **C.** hearing

4. Which action is helpful to bats?

   **A.** growing plants that bloom at night
   **B.** using pesticides to kill insects
   **C.** closing dangerous caves and mines

*Answer key on page 32.*

# GLOSSARY

**clotting**
Sticking together to form a thick mass.

**color-blind**
Unable to tell certain colors apart.

**ecosystems**
The collections of living things in different natural areas.

**fertilizer**
A substance that helps plants grow.

**hedgerows**
Rows of trees or shrubs that grow around or between fields.

**hibernating**
Resting or sleeping through the winter.

**nectar**
A sweet liquid released by plants.

**predator**
An animal that hunts other animals for food.

**prey**
An animal that is hunted and eaten by a different animal.

**species**
Groups of animals or plants that are similar.

# TO LEARN MORE

## BOOKS

Hibbert, Clare. *Bat Hospital*. New York: PowerKids Press, 2015.

Markle, Sandra. *The Case of the Vanishing Little Brown Bats: A Scientific Mystery*. Minneapolis: Millbrook Press, 2015.

Niver, Heather Moore. *Vampire Bats After Dark*. New York: Enslow Publishing, 2016.

## NOTE TO EDUCATORS

Visit **www.focusreaders.com** to find lesson plans, activities, links, and other resources related to this title.

# INDEX

**Answer Key: 1.** Answers will vary; **2.** Answers will vary; **3.** C; **4.** A